YOUR KNOWLEDGE HAS

Bibliographic information published by the German National Library:

The German National Library lists this publication in the National Bibliography; detailed bibliographic data are available on the Internet at http://dnb.dnb.de .

Imprint:

Copyright © 2018 GRIN Verlag
Print and binding: Books on Demand GmbH, Norderstedt Germany
ISBN: 9783668689961

This book at GRIN:

https://www.grin.com/document/421249

Abdallah Ziraba, Chinedum Okolo

The Impact of Information Technology (IT) Policies and Strategies to Organization's Competitive Advantage

A Case Study of the ICT University

GRIN Verlag

GRIN - Your knowledge has value

Since its foundation in 1998, GRIN has specialized in publishing academic texts by students, college teachers and other academics as e-book and printed book. The website www.grin.com is an ideal platform for presenting term papers, final papers, scientific essays, dissertations and specialist books.

Visit us on the internet:

http://www.grin.com/

http://www.facebook.com/grincom

http://www.twitter.com/grin_com

THE IMPACT OF IT POLICIES AND STRATEGIES TO ORGANIZATION'S COMPETITIVE
ADVANTAGE. A CASE STUDY OF THE ICT UNIVERSITY.

Authors:

1) Abdallah Ziraba, lecturer ICT Department.

The ICT University Yaounde Cameroon,

2) *Chinedum Okolo, Scholar and Researcher. ICT Department. The ICT University Yaounde*

Cameroon

Contents

1

ABSTRACT

The paper aims at reviewing the importance and various aspects of Information Technology (IT) policy and strategy formulation as well as the impacts of IT policy and strategy for competitive advantage in the organization. The paper reveals that information technology which is a vital too used for a more effective and efficient communication, is advancing at great pace at and poses great threat to organizations and employees right of privacy. The paper upholds that IT policy formulation is one of the best ways, to ensure effective IT standards, procedures, that protects organizational IT resources and controls information sharing. The article goes further to show how IT strategy formulation helps organization (using the *Information and Communication Technology University* as a case study) to achieve its set objectives through policies which controls mission critical activities. The Authors reviewed a total of 23 peer reviewed articles from prominent journals. The article addressed the following sections: *The topic, abstract, introduction, literature review as well as summarized concepts of IT policy and strategy, Importance of IT strategy for business competitive advantage, discussions of organizational IT strategies with case study, impacts of IT policy and strategy on organization, purpose of IT policy and strategy in the organization, summary and conclusions/findings.* The study revealed that IT strategy formulation offers six key advantages which are; Creation of new IT services or products, Improved or quick decision making, Customer and supplier intimacy, Operational excellence, Competitive advantage, and Business survival. The ICT University was used as a case study. The study concluded that IT policies and strategies must align with the organization's vision, mission critical activities, in order to realize set objectives. It was recommended that any organization that succeed, should first set visions, adopt IT strategies, formulate IT policies in order to have a good sense of business direction for competitive advantage.

INTRODUCTION

In accordance to (Kalpana Mathur, Akanksha, Berwa, 2017), Information Technology (IT) is advancing at a great pace. This advancement poses great threat to organization and businesses. Information sharing using technology, is a mission critical activity in the organization. This is because the technology adopted for information sharing and the controls put in place determines the survival of any business or organization. Consequently, the use of information technology must be guided by IT policies with strategic objectives. The purpose of IT policy is to protect the dynamic valuable resources of an enterprise. This is done, through the formulation of appropriate policies, strategies, procedures, standards, and guidelines.

It is important to access the business needs, adopt suitable technologies, and set policies, and strategies. In view of (Christine, Holyland A., Kevin, Adams M., Andreas Tolk, Li Xu D., 2014), policy and strategy must not be in conflict with organization's mission and vision. This implies that, policies and strategies must align with the business vision and mission (Llanos Cuena, Andres Boza, Angel Ortiz, 2011). Therefore, this paper examined the importance of IT policies and strategies for business competitive advantage using the ICT University, Yaoundé Cameroon as a case study.

IT POLICY: According to (Tripwire Guest Authors, 2017), Policy is an elite statement requirements that is binding through standards, which is been carried out through procedures. The (University college Cork, Ireland, 2012) defined policy as a high-level of overall IT plan

3

that covers the general goals and rules on how to exploit information technology and data within the University, the IT policy sets a path in which IT resources are utilized. Pointing to (Wanganui District Council, 2010) definition of policy; policy is a well-designed and constructive statement of position on an ongoing matter or duty that guides any response or action, and has been adopted by resolution by a body or institution. A policy is a broad statement that outlines the government's major goals and concern, that works hand in hand with the country's constitution and can be applied to a particular sector (e.g. primary education sector policy) or narrowed down specifically to a sub-sector (e.g. primary education) which points to a definite issue (e.g. teachers enrollment). A policy defines a particular position, aiming to explore solutions to an issue, which will serve as a guide for users of the policy to meet up with the target of the institution. (UNESCO Bangkok, 2013). The (Office of the Associate Director for Policy, 2015) Policy is a regulation, procedure, administrative action, spur or voluntary practice of governments and other institutions. Policy decisions help in application, distribution, and utilization for resource allocations. Policies in many ways influence the health sectors and sub-sectors various ways especially in the aspect of public health. Additionally, (University Of West London, 2017) Defined information security policy as an approach to the management of information which serves as a guiding principle and responsibilities necessary to protect the information system of the University in which all students and staff members shall abide by it.

With a critical assessment of the above definitions of IT policy (or Policy) from various authors: (Office of the Associate Director for Policy, 2015), (Tripwire Guest Authors, 2017) and (University Of West London, 2017) view policy as a documented statement in which people that work or function in an institution or organization are obliged to adhere to, regularly in process of policy carrying out decisions regarding the division or subdivision of an institution or organization. Therefore, we can infer that the three authors share a common perspective. Conclusively, IT policies for end-user equipment is defined as a framework document of rules or procedures, standards and guidelines which directs the routine IT affairs of an organization.

PROCEDURES: According to the (Asia Pacific International College, 2016) defines procedure in purpose statement as guidelines for the administration of information technology resources and assets within its institution. Furthermore, procedures are detailed step-by-step activities or processes that should be performed to achieve a certain purpose. That is they spell out how the policy and the supporting standards will actually be executed in an operating environment (University college Cork, Ireland, 2012). Haven reviewed the literature above, in simple term procedure can be seen as a well-defined rules and regulations which guides the use of IT in the organization.

STANDARDS: The (University college Cork, Ireland, 2012), asserts standards a documentation which provide some directives that ensure that specific technologies and business applications are used in a certain manner across the University to meet a defined or set goal. Standards regulate how hardware and software products are to be used. In summary, standard refer to mandatory controls that governs the all IT resources (both hardware and software usage) in the organization.

GUIDELINES: Following (University college Cork, Ireland, 2012), guidelines is a target that streamline particular procedures according to a set repetitive or sound practice. From its definition, following a guideline is never mandatory. Distinctively guidelines in contrast to standards, guidelines refers to a non-mandatory control or best practices pointing at specific IT processes, operations, and resources.

IT STRATEGY: According to (Wanganui District Council, 2010), strategy is a set general trend set for the organization or institution to achieve an anticipated goal, which comprises the necessary phases to get to reach the target. In addition, the target to be met can either be a long-term or short-term target. (Zelenkov, 2015) Explains IT strategy as a long term comprehensive plan which helps an organization to actualize its set objectives through the adoption of suitable technologies, processes, and creation of new services or products and models, as well as modification of existing ones for business continuity and competitive edge. Examples of strategy includes; partnership, diversification and innovation. Following (Mekhala, 2016), information technology (IT) strategic plan is a document that specifies the comprehensive information technology(IT)-enabled business management practices an organization uses to guide its operations. It represents a guide as to how decisions that are related to IT in the organization made, carried out and applied to tasks using the plan as a charter. In view of (Nikols, 2016), he defines and gives insight on strategy as a group of complex network of ideas, perceptions, goals, knowledge, and prospects that provides a guidance for a particular action in order to meet up with a particular target. He further explained strategy as a general framework that provides guidance for actions that will be carried out and, at the same time, is fashioned by the actions taken. From an aspect of information system (IS) strategy, (Daniel Q. Chen, Martin Mocker, & David S. Pretson, Alexander Teubner, 2010) define information system strategy as standpoint or perspective of an organization or institution on the investment in, deployment, use, and management in order to achieve an effective or efficient running of the information system. (Neelambal M. Govender & Marius Pretorius , 2015) Described strategy as a plan that

6

organizations intend to trail in order to achieve certain desired objectives that offer an advantage over their rivals. More importantly, it refers to the organization's aims and the activities it pursues to attain a sustained existence to clinch its market environment.

After reviewing (Mekhala, 2016) and (Nikols, 2016), they both agree and state that IT Strategy sets a guide on how decisions regarding IT are carried out within an organization. They also share the same view by stating that, IT Strategy gives a sense of direction for a good running of an organization in order for it to reach its target or objectives. However, (Mekhala, 2016) and (Zelenkov, 2015), describe IT Strategy in common by sustaining that IT strategy is a well thought and designed (or comprehensive) IT management proposal that serves a means to reach a particular purpose.

IMPORTANCE OF IT STRATEGY FOR COMPETITIVE ADVANTAGE

In modern times, IT strategy formulation has been found to be the backbone for the survival of any new or existing business. This entails that any organization that will flourish or have cutting-edge over others must st rategize periodically. According to (Laudon, Kenneth C., Laudon Jane P., 2015) IT strategy is important for the following basic reasons:

- Creation of new IT services or products
- Improved or quick decision making
- Customer and supplier intimacy
- Operational excellence
- Competitive advantage
- Business survival

7

Creation of new IT services or products: for any business to thrive today, it is important to create new IT products or services. For instance, (Johnson Katherine, Li Yang, Phan Hang, Singer Jason, Trinh Hoang, 2012) asserted that, Apple Incorporated changed the music world, through an IT strategy. This strategy changed the distribution of music from CDs, tapes, cassettes, and other digital contents through the use of third-party digital content delivery system of legal online distribution of not only music, but applications and as well as other digital contents based on its iTunes technology strategy. The company has also included innovative IT strategic distribution of books with the innovation of iBook store for sales and purchases of books via the same iTunes platform services as well. .

Improved or quick decision making: initially, companies were relying on the traditional methods of getting customer feedback or complaints about products and services provided which required physical contact with the customers. Conversely, in recent times IT companies have adopted modern IT strategies through provision of digital dashboard, which gives real-time information on customer's complaints or challenges and as well offers rapid solution. For example, Hp has integrated a digitalized platform where customers can lay their complaints and response is given to the customers immediately. This can help the company to understand some of the lapses in their products and services, thereby immediate corrective measures are taken for better customer experience.

Customer and supplier intimacy: nowadays, nearly all sectors are in close contact with their customers through a reliable application of IT Strategy. The bank customers receives immediate bank transaction alerts via e-mails and short message services (sms). Those in the tourist sector are not left out, as travelers now get immediate travel updates, online hotel or flight booking reservation are now available for the customers even from their bedrooms. Suppliers to shopping malls can now get inventory alerts and know when to supply products.

Operational excellence: in order to improve operational efficiency, satisfy customers and maximize profits, businesses set IT strategies by adopting suitable technologies that meets the business needs. For example the use of a disruptive technology like automated teller machines (ATM) in the banking industry, customers no longer need to queue up for a long time in order to withdraw money. The ATM serve the customers more efficiently and effectively in little or no time, thereby servicing more customers in less time even during weekends or public holidays.

Competitive advantage: when there are new IT products and services, improved decision making, customer and supplier intimacy, and operational excellence achieved, these results to an organization having a competitive advantage over other. Competitive advantage is achieved when an organization is using a good technology that others are not using. For example, ICT University Cameroon uses online platform for lecture delivery. This is a distinctive strategy, because it is a strategy that is not easily copied. In Africa as a whole only few Universities, offer similar services. This IT strategy gives ICT University a competitive advantage over other universities.

Business survival: an organization that has achieved competitive advantage can therefor flourish and survive competition. This is only achievable, through suitable IT strategies.

According to   (Taper, 2014) on the importance of strategic management to business organization, he stated that an effective strategy formulation and implementation play a vital role in crafting the processes and procedures of an organization which will also bring about positive impact on income growth, earnings, and return on investment. He further buttressed his point by

9

explaining that (Arthur Thompson, John Gamble E., Strickland A.J., 2007) affirmed that an acceptable and great thought out strategy may be management's prescription to finishing business, its guide will focused advantage, its course of action for pleasing clients Furthermore enhancing monetary execution.

DISCUSSIONS ON ORGANIZATIONAL IT STRATEGY (A CASE THE ICT UNIVERSITY)

Every organization seeks to increase its capacity and to be in existence for as long as it can be. The claim by (Mian M. Ajmal, Mehmood Khan, Matloub Hussain, & Peri Helo, 2017) showed that one of the major aspirations of most (if not all) businesses, is to attain high level of sustainability and survival. To attain sustainability and survival, it is important to point out that strategy plays a part in the attainment of these potentials. As earlier stated above by (Llanos Cuena, Andres Boza, Angel Ortiz, 2011); strategy has to align (or be in line) with the mission and vision of the organization. For us to effectively discuss about the strategies we need to examine the organizations mission and vision statement. (Abdullah H. Alharty, Hamad Rashid, Romano Pagiari,& Faisal Khan, 2017) Affirmed that, there are two vital phases of strategy which are: formation and execution which shape the overall success or failure of an organization, and they change almost the whole dynamics of the organization. Furthermore, the strategy will have a good sense of direction, if policies are put in place which will serve as guide for the realization of the organizations objectives (or target). In view of strategy implementation (Abdullah H. Alharty, Hamad Rashid, Romano Pagiari,& Faisal Khan, 2017) Indicated that a good strategy has great influence on the life and future of any organization and so it is necessary that the strategy is designed critically and implemented for survival and continuity. In a lighter and very

10

important note, (Neelambal M. Govender & Marius Pretorius , 2015) concluded that, the strategy approach required for ICT adoption is one that can potentially address instability experienced in the modern-day environment, whilst being responsive and flexible to react to the business needs. In this review, the ICT University shall be reviewed as a case study. Some major discussions on aspects of the IT strategy adopted by other organizations (or institutions), and how it can be embraced by the ICT University to bring about competitiveness for its institution.

Information and communication technology (ICT) is present almost everywhere in our high-end technological and globalized society (Khalid, Saifuddin and Pedersen, Mette Jun Lykkegaard, 2016). To get a better understanding of the aspects that shall be deliberated, it is important to get a basic understanding of Information and communication technology (ICT). Information and communication technologies consist of hardware, software, network and media for collecting, storing, processing, transmitting and presenting information (such as voice, data, text and image) and other related services. ICT is consists of two major components namely: information and communication infrastructure (ICI) and information technology (IT) (Sogol Talebiana, Hamid Movahed Mohammadia & Ahmad Rezvanfara, 2014). The potential incorporating ICT to help people learn has not been largely observed until recently. Tutors are beginning to understand the potential for technology to help students construct meaning for themselves based on learning activities (Tongkaw, 2013). However, (Tagreed Kattoua, Musa Al-Lozi & Ala'aldin Alrowwad, 2016) revealed that due to the swift growth of internet technology, universities around the world are investing heavily in e-learning systems to support their customary teaching and to improve their students' learning experience and performance. The use of ICT in education has hugely reformed learning and teaching processes. Furthermore, it has stretched new opportunities for

11

learning and accessing to educational resources beyond those customarily means of learning and teaching process (Sogol Talebiana, Hamid Movahed Mohammadia & Ahmad Rezvanfara, 2014). Intensive adoption of these modern trends of technology in education by the ICT University early enough will serve as a major strategy, which will go a long way in fostering a competitive edge over other universities around the world, especially in developing nations of Africa. The challenges that may be faced by the ICT University in terms of competitiveness can either be an internal or external factor. These factors in line with (Tongkaw, 2013) include: policies, politics, culture and general lack of support from government which are deep seated and will need strong and consistent activism to bring about educational reformation. Therefore, the enlisted factors above will either foster or impede the adaptation or implementation of ICT in education depending on how they are handled and prioritized, particularly regarding schools that have interest to acclimate ICT into their system. The presence of ICT will not bring about competitiveness this is because not all firms have similar resources. The resources may become a source of competitive advantage, if they are valuable or rare, imitable, and not substitutable without great effort, and if the firm succeeds in offering a special services to its customers or clients (Tanja Mihalic, Daniela Garbrin Pranicevic & Josip Americ, 2015). In addition to this, the ICT University adopting new trends of education mode of knowledge transfer (that is through implementation ICT) should customize her services in such a way that it will bridge the gaps of other competitors that have also acclimated IT within its mode of package delivery. The main aim of conveying tailored services into the institution or organization will be to bring a great strategic means of attaining competitiveness, survival and continuity. As stated above, the importance of strategy for competitiveness is for business survival. Some strategic planning that will bring about a swift (or speedy) growth of in terms of competitiveness may include: fast and

12

available internet connectivity (for smooth running of the ICT resources); Digitalized library loaded with sufficient electronic books (to foster research); well and improved e-learning platforms (for online classes, conferences and seminars); enhanced and well secured database (for data storage, processing and retrieval); and a modern and well-furnished IT laboratories (for practical and enhanced learning/studies). With the facilities mentioned above, if implemented by the ICT University will make the institution to stand out and thrive better within its environs. The use of ICT is a symbol of a new era in education. Similarly, ICT modifies thought patterns, enriches existing educational models and provides new training models. These models shares features of a technology-based training and suggest new learning methods in which the learner plays an active role and also emphasizes self-directed, autonomous, flexible and interactive learning process (Sogol Talebiana, Hamid Movahed Mohammadia & Ahmad Rezvanfara, 2014). Finally, from a critical review and assessment of various literature above, it won't be wrong to infer that ICT has played a very vital role as to operational and functional management in organizations. Thus, initiation of ICT into organizations has proven to be a major strategic means of eradicating the gaps experienced in the customary means of setting up strategies (or IT strategies) for effective and efficient running of any organization in modern times.

IMPACTS OF IT POLICY AND STRATEGY ON AN ORGANIZATION

(Healey David, Mecker Sacha, Antia Usen, Cottle Edward, 2016), in an attempt to counter cybercrime in the organization, particularly in the energy sector reviewed the existing European IT policies and reported that IT policy and strategy must be given a serious attention. The following six recommendations were made;

13

- **Appointment of central authority:** It was stated that IT policies should be formulated, implemented, in legislation to become European Union (EU) Law. In addition, it was recommended that a central authority should be appointed for an executive role to ensure compliance.

- **Information sharing:** It was recommended that synergy should be made a priority in the organization. This means, taking information sharing as a best practice.

- **Incident reporting:** The study recommended that all stake holders should coordinate incident reporting and share data of observed related attacks.

- **Security standards:** It was stated that a minimum security standard be applied in all cases of information sharing with the use of digital devices and other means.

- **Alignment of cybersecurity activities:** This requires all stakeholders' activities to be aligned and integrated with national cybersecurity strategic operations.

- **Certification board:** The study recommended the creation of a certification board for cybersecurity certification and to provide oversight and support for national cybersecurity certifications.

The above suggested approach is the best of its kind. This approach will be very helpful in ensuring effective information sharing and general IT controls among stakeholders. More so, (Gouardères, 2017), explores the development of IT development policies and defensive strategies and affirms that it is important to appoint a central body and empower them to effectively implement best practices, such as mandatory reporting of security attacks and information sharing. This procedure will achieve an optimum result. This is simply because, all parties are pointing towards information sharing across stakeholders. Hence, they admitted that IT policy and strategy is important and must be communicated to all that will be affected by the policy.

(Michael Johnson, Elizabeth, Shewood-Randall, 2015), reported that globally, people rely on digital technology to collect, share, and store information that enables research and boost security and efficiency in operations. It was affirmed that effective information sharing, requires standards, procedures, and best practices (policy), alongside with a well-defined strategy. In addition, it was reviewed that, developing and implementing appropriate organization's IT policies reduce the risk of cyber threats. It was further stated that, IT controls and strategies must be put in place to accelerate cyber threat notifications for appropriate counter measure.

PURPOSE OF IT POLICY AND STRATEGY IN THE ORGANIZATION

(Thomas, 2001), on risk analysis in the organization, examined the need for management IT controls and procedures. It was stated that the purpose of IT policy, is to protect valuable resources of an organization, such as hardware, software, and the people. It was further reported that the selection of appropriate IT policies and strategies helps an organization to meet its business objectives or mission. This is done by protecting, the employees, organization reputation, legal position, financial resources, all tangible assets and intangible assets.

As reported by (EduMinRwanda, 2016), IT strategy and policy in education helps to increase access to basic education for both formal and informal education. IT ensures the provision of reliable IT tools for learning, researching, teaching and information sharing. It was affirmed that, a good IT policy and strategy promotes an independent and lifelong learning from basic to tertiary education. It was further stated that, IT policy and strategy supports evidence decision making, with regards to strategic planning, policy review and implementation, monitoring and evaluation, and resource allocation.

SUMMARY

This literature review expounds the impact of IT policy and strategy to organizations in enhancing competitiveness. The review covers some major themes such as: Definition of IT policy and strategy, The importance of IT policy for competitive advantage, Discussion of organizational IT Strategy, Impacts of IT policy and strategy, and Purpose of IT policy and strategy. However, we shall briefly review what other authors and co-authors' point of view of each theme, try to fill the gap and appreciate their contributions where necessary.

From the definitions of *IT policy* by (Office of the Associate Director for Policy, 2015), (Tripwire Guest Authors, 2017) and (University Of West London, 2017) IT policy is a documented statement which is binding upon a group of people in an organization before activities or decisions regarding the use of IT tools and infrastructure are taken in an organization. From this definition, we can infer that before any action is taken care must be taken by users of the IT infrastructure so as not to deviate from the procedures and standards set by the organization regarding the use of IT in the organization. However, it is worth noting that some policies may turn obsolete with time, as a result of the fast evolution of technologies in IT. Additionally, we can state IT policy as a constantly updated document which meets and maintains a steady guidelines, procedures and standards in taking decisions regarding the use of IT infrastructures by end users of an organization.

The *IT strategy* which is another important factor in enhancing competitiveness is concisely and critically reviewed by authors and co-authors vis-à-vis their perspective of IT strategy and compared to give a conclusive view on the subject matter. Reviewing the definitions given by: (Wanganui District Council, 2010), (Zelenkov, 2015), (Mekhala, 2016) and (Daniel Q. Chen, Martin Mocker, & David S. Pretson, Alexander Teubner, 2010) IT strategy is a set of well thought document that sets to give a guide or means using IT on how to meet an organizations target or objectives. Emphatically, (Nikols, 2016) defines IT strategy as an intricate network of ideas, insights, goals, and forecasts that an IT framework that gives a sense of direction for actions to be carried out in an organization. In summary, IT strategy will be best well-defined as an intensively compiled, sensitive and essential document that covers an ample and a well-planned means used to reach a stipulated objective by an organization through the use of some suitable IT framework or resources in order to meet up with the projected target.

From the definition of *IT strategy* we can see and identify its *importance for competitiveness* of any organization or business. These strategies must be dynamic such that it is unique particularly when carrying out sensitive decisions in the organization. In view of (Laudon, Kenneth C., Laudon Jane P., 2015) on the importance of IT strategy, the following briefly highlights these importance: creation of new products and services; healthier and swift response when carrying out verdicts; good relationship between clients and their suppliers; operational excellence; competitive advantage, and survival of the business. In addition, most (or every) organization or business desires to expand tremendously. Following these importance of IT strategy, it is evident that IT strategy is a very important factor that fosters the growth as well as increased productivity.

In view of discussing *IT strategies in an organization, in which the ICT University was taken as a case study.* A critical review of the subject matter lead to a major understanding of the concept and the findings in which it was discovered that intensive adoption of these modern trends of technology in education by the ICT University early enough will serve as a major strategy, which will go a long way in fostering a competitive edge over other universities around the world, especially in developing nations of Africa. These models shares features of a technology-based training and suggest new learning methods in which the learner plays an active role and also emphasizes self-directed, autonomous, flexible and interactive learning process (Sogol Talebiana, Hamid Movahed Mohammadia & Ahmad Rezvanfara, 2014). (Abdullah H. Alharty, Hamad Rashid, Romano Pagiari,& Faisal Khan, 2017) Affirmed that, there are two vital phases of strategy which are: formation and execution which shape the overall success or failure of an organization, and they change almost the whole dynamics of the organization. However, (Tagreed Kattoua, Musa Al-Lozi & Ala'aldin Alrowwad, 2016), revealed that due to the swift growth of internet technology, universities all over the world have plunged investments into adoption e-learning systems to enhance the teaching and learning experience. Learning and educational resources are now at a very close proximity, and more flexible as compared to the traditional educational platform (Sogol Talebiana, Hamid Movahed Mohammadia & Ahmad Rezvanfara, 2014).

IT policy and strategy have a great deal of *impacts on an organization*, especially in fast growth of IT and globalization in the world of today. Development of IT policies and defensive strategies is important to appoint a central body and empower them to effectively implement best practices (Gouardères, 2017). This procedure will achieve a prime result. This is simply because, all parties are pointing towards information exchange across stakeholders. Hence, they admitted that IT policy and strategy is important and must be communicated to all that will be affected by the policy. (Michael Johnson, Elizabeth, Shewood-Randall, 2015), reported that globally, people rely on digital technology to collect, share, and store information that enables research and boost security and efficiency in operations. It was acknowledged that effective information sharing, requires standards, procedures, and best practices (policy), alongside with a well-defined strategy are very vital in operations within any organization.

The purpose of IT policy and strategy in an organization is to protect valuable resources of an organization, such as hardware, software, and the people. Additionally, the choice of appropriate IT policies and strategies will help an organization in attainment of its objectives or mission. As reported by (EduMinRwanda, 2016), IT policy and strategy enables higher chances of access to basic education. It was also admitted that, a good IT policy and strategy promotes an independent and lifelong learning from basic to tertiary education. Finally, IT policy and strategy supports decision making, with regards to strategic planning; policy review and implementation; monitoring and evaluation, and resource allocation.

CONCLUSION

IT policy and strategy formulation is important in any organization. The policies and strategies must align with the organization's vision, mission in order to realize its objectives. Therefore, any organization that must succeed, should first set visions, adopt IT strategies, formulate IT policies in order to have a good sense of business direction for competitive advantage.

REFERENCES:

Daniel Q. Chen, Martin Mocker, & David S. Pretson, Alexander Teubner. (2010). Information Systems Strategy: Reconceptualization, Measurement, and Imlications. *MIS Quarterly*, 233-259.

Office of the Associate Director for Policy. (2015). Definition Of Policy. *Centre for Disease Control and Prevention.*

Abdullah H. Alharty, Hamad Rashid, Romano Pagiari,& Faisal Khan. (2017). Identification of Strategy Implementation Influencing Factors and Their Effects on the perfomance. *International Journal of Business and Social Science*, 35-36.

Arthur Thompson, John Gamble E., Strickland A.J. (2007). *Crafting and Executing Strategy*. New York: McGrawHill Irwin.

Asia Pacific International College. (2016, December 16). INFORMATION TECHNOLOGY ADMINISTRATION PROCEDURES. *Information Technology Administration Procedures*, p. 2.

Centers for Centers for Disease Control and Prevention, Office of the Associate Director for Policy. (2015). Definition of Policy. *CDC Policy Process.*

Christine, Holyland A., Kevin, Adams M., Andreas Tolk, Li Xu D. (2014). The RQ-Tech methodology: a new paradigm for conceptualizing strategic enterprise architectures. *Journal of Management Analytics*, 55-77.

EduMinRwanda. (2016). *ICT in Education Policy*. Available on: http://mineduc.gov.rw/fileadmin/user_upload/pdf_files/ICT_in_Education_Policy_approved.pdf .

Gouardères, F. (2017, March). AT A GLANCE for the ITRE committee Study in focus. *Cyber Security Strategy for the Energy sector*, http://www.europarl.europa.eu/RegData/etudes/ATAG/2017/602019/IPOL_ATA(2017)602019_EN.pdf.

Healey David, Mecker Sacha, Antia Usen, Cottle Edward. (2016). *Cyber Security Strategy for the Energy Sector.* http://www.europarl.europa.eu/RegData/etudes/STUD/2016/587333/IPOL_STU(2016)587333_EN.pdf.

Intel IT Center. (2012). Cloud Computing Research for IT Strategic Planning. *Peer Research*, 4-5.

it, I. (n.d.).

Johnson Katherine, Li Yang, Phan Hang, Singer Jason, Trinh Hoang. (2012). The Innovative Success that is Apple. *Theses, Dissertion and Capstones*, 418.

Kalpana Mathur, Akanksha, Berwa. (2017). Sustainable competitiveness: redefining the future with technology and innovation. *Journal of Sustainable Finance and Investment*, 290-306.

Khalid, Saifuddin and Pedersen, Mette Jun Lykkegaard. (2016). Digital exclusion in higher education contexts: A systematic literature review. *Procedia- Social and Behavioral Sciences*, 614-621.

Laudon, Kenneth C., Laudon Jane P. (2015). Management Information System: Managing the Digital Firm. In L. J. Laudon Kenneth C., *Management Information System: Managing the Digital Firm.*

Llanos Cuena, Andres Boza, Angel Ortiz. (2011). An enterprise engineering approach for the alignment of business and information technology strategy. *International Journal Of Computer Integrated Manufacturing*, 974-992.

Mekhala. (2016, August 22). *Business and ERP.* Retrieved from Tech Target Network: http://searchcio.techtarget.com/definition/IT-strategy-information-technology-strategy

Mian M. Ajmal, Mehmood Khan, Matloub Hussain, & Peri Helo. (2017). Conceptualizing and incorporating social sustainability in the business world. *International Journal of Sustainable Development & World Ecology*, 327-339.

Michael Johnson, Elizabeth, Shewood-Randall. (2015). Cyber Strategy. *US Department of Energy.*

Neelambal M. Govender & Marius Pretorius . (2015). A critcal analysis of information and communications technology adoption: The strategy as practice perspective. *Acta commercii*, 1.

Nikols, F. (2016). Strayegy. *Strategy and Meanings*, 8.

Sogol Talebiana, Hamid Movahed Mohammadia & Ahmad Rezvanfara. (2014). Information and communication technology (ICT) in higher education: advantages, disadvantages, conveniences and limitations of applying e-learning to agricultural students in Iran. *Procedia - Social and Behavioral Sciences*, 300-305.

Tagreed Kattoua, Musa Al-Lozi & Ala'aldin Alrowwad. (2016). A Review of Literature on E-Learning Systems in Higher Education. *International Journal of Business Management and Economic Research*, 754-762.

Tanja Mihalic, Daniela Garbrin Pranicevic & Josip Arneric. (2015). The changing role of ICT competitiveness: the case of the Slovenian hotel sector. *Economic Research*, 367-383.

Taper, J. (2014). *The Importance of Strategic Management to Business Organizations*, 122-131.

The ICT University. (n.d.). *About ICTU.* Retrieved from The ICT University: https://ictuniversity.org/mission-and-vision/

The IOWA State University. (n.d., n.d. n.d.). *About.* Retrieved from IOWA State University: https://www.policy.iastate.edu/itacceptableuse

Thomas, P. R. (2001). *Information Security Policies, Procedures, and Standards: Guidelines for Effective Information Security Management.* Auerbach Publications.

Tongkaw, A. (2013). Multi perspective integrations Information and Communication Technologies (ICTs) in higher education in developing countries: case study Thailand. *Procedia - Social and Behavioral Sciences* , 1468-1469.

21

Tripwire Guest Authors. (2017, November 27). Understanding Policies, Control Objectives, Standards, Guidelines & Procedures. *The State of Security.*

UNESCO Bangkok. (2013). UNESCO Handbok on Education Policy Analysis and Programming. *Education Policy Analysis*, 7.

University college Cork, Ireland. (2012, November 11). IT policy Framework. *IT Policy Framework*, p. 4.

University Of West London. (2017, December 4). Information Security Policy. p. 5.

Wahamala, F. (2011). *ITU National Cybersecurity Strategy Guide*, 99-100.

Wanganui District Council. (2010, October 29). *Strategy and Policy Guideline.* Retrieved from Whanganui District Council: http://www.whanganui.govt.nz/our-council/publications/policies/Documents/Strategy-PolicyGuidelines.pdf

Zelenkov, Y. (2015). Critical regular components of IT strategy: Decision making model and efficiency measurement. *Journal of Management Analytics*, 95 - 110.

YOUR KNOWLEDGE HAS VALUE

- We will publish your bachelor's and master's thesis, essays and papers

- Your own eBook and book - sold worldwide in all relevant shops

- Earn money with each sale

Upload your text at www.GRIN.com
and publish for free